W9-ATR-962

CONTEMPORARY AMERICAN SUCCESS STORIES

Famous People of Hispanic Heritage

Volume VII

Barbara Marvis
Melanie Cole
Tony Cantu

A Mitchell Lane
Multicultural Biography Series
• Celebrating Diversity •

CONTEMPORARY AMERICAN SUCCESS STORIES
Famous People of Hispanic Heritage

Publisher's Cataloging in Publication
Marvis, Barbara, Melanie Cole, and Tony Cantu.
    Famous people of Hispanic heritage. Vol. VII / Barbara Marvis, Melanie Cole, and Tony Cantu.
    p. cm. —(Contemporary American success stories)—(A Mitchell Lane multicultural biography series)
    Includes index.
    LCCN: 95-75963
    ISBN: 1-883845-40-8 (hc)
    ISBN: 1-883845-39-4 (pbk)

    1. Hispanic Americans—Biography—Juvenile literature. I. Title. II. Series.

E184.S75M37 1997   920'.009268

QBI96-20404

Illustrated by Barbara Tidman
Project Editor: Susan R. Scarfe

Mitchell Lane
PUBLISHERS

Your Path To Quality Educational Material
P.O. Box 200
Childs, Maryland 21916-0200

TABLE OF CONTENTS

Acknowledgments

Every reasonable effort has been made to gain copyright permission where such permission has been deemed necessary. Any oversight brought to the publisher's attention will be corrected in future printings.

Most of the stories in this series were written through personal interviews and/or with the complete permission of the person, representative of the person, or family of the person being profiled and are authorized biographies. Though we attempted to contact each person profiled within, for various reasons we were unable to authorize every story. All stories have been thoroughly researched and checked for accuracy, and to the best of our knowledge represent true stories.

Our greatest appreciation goes to Merel Julia (telephone interview February 6, 1997, and others with author Barbara Marvis) and Susan Wright for their help with the story and photographs of Raul Julia; Andres Galarraga (telephone interview April 1997 with author Tony Cantu) and Fernando Cuza for help with our story about Andres Galarraga.

Photograph Credits

The quality of the photographs in this book may vary; many of them are personal snapshots supplied to us courtesy of the person being profiled. Many are very old, one-of-a-kind photos. Most are not professional photographs, nor were they intended to be. The publisher felt that the personal nature of the stories in this book would only be enhanced by real-life, family album–type photos, and chose to include many interesting snapshots, even if they were not quite the best quality. Cover illustration: Barbara Tidman; pp. 8, 26, 48, 66 sketch by Barbara Tidman; pp. 11, 13, 14, 20, 21, 23 courtesy Merel Julia; p. 18 Tim Boxer, Archive Photos; p. 24 Reuters/Corbis-Bettmann; pp. 36, 39 Reuters/Corbis-Bettmann; p. 41 Archive Photos; p. 23 AP Photos; p. 44 James M. Kelley, Globe Photos; p. 52 Otto Greule Jr., Allsport; p. 54 UPI/Corbis-Bettmann; p. 59, 65 Stephen Dunn, Allsport; p. 60, 62, 64 courtesy Fernando Cuza; p. 63 Tim Defrisco, Allsport; pp. 71, 81, 84, 94 courtesy T-V Enterprises, Ltd.; p. 82 Reuters/Corbis-Bettmann; p. 87 Archive Photos; p. 89 AP Photo, Franz Neumayr; pp. 90, 92 AP Photo, Elise Amendola

About the Authors

Barbara Marvis has been a professional writer for nearly twenty years. Motivated by her own experience with ethnic discrimination as a young Jewish girl growing up in suburban Philadelphia, Ms. Marvis developed the **Contemporary American Success Stories** series to dispel racial and ethnic prejudice, to tell culturally diverse stories that maintain ethnic and racial distinction, and to provide positive role models for young minorities. She is the author of several books for young adults, including the series **Famous People of Asian Ancestry** and **Tommy Nuñez: NBA Referee/Taking My Best Shot**.

Melanie Cole has been a writer and editor for seventeen years. She has been an associate editor of *Texas Monthly* and is now managing editor of *Hispanic* magazine.

Tony Cantu is a bilingual freelance writer based in Princeton, New Jersey. He is a contributing writer to *Hispanic* magazine.

INTRODUCTION

by Kathy Escamilla

One of the fastest growing ethno-linguistic groups in the United States is a group of people who are collectively called Hispanic. The term *Hispanic* is an umbrella term that encompasses people from many nationalities, from all races, and from many social and cultural groups. The label *Hispanic* sometimes obscures the diversity of people who come from different countries and speak different varieties of Spanish. Therefore, it is crucial to know that the term *Hispanic* encompasses persons whose origins are from Spanish-speaking countries, including Spain, Mexico, Central and South America, Cuba, Puerto Rico, the Dominican Republic, and the United States. It is important also to note that Spanish is the heritage language of most Hispanics. However, Hispanics living in the United States are also linguistically diverse. Some speak mostly Spanish and little English, others are bilingual, and some speak only English.

Hispanics are often also collectively called Latinos. In addition to calling themselves Hispanics or Latinos, many people in this group also identify themselves in more specific terms according to their country of origin or their ethnic group (e.g., Cuban-American, Chicano, Puerto Rican-American, etc.). The population of Hispanics in the United States is expected to triple in the next twenty-five years, making it imperative that students in schools understand and appreciate the enormous contributions that persons of Hispanic heritage have made in the Western Hemisphere in general and in the United States in particular.

There are many who believe that in order to be successful in the United States now and in the twenty-first century, all persons from diverse cultural backgrounds, such as Hispanics, should be assimilated. To be assimilated means losing one's distinct cultural and linguistic heritage and changing to or adopting the cultural attributes of the dominant culture.

Others disagree with the assimilationist viewpoint and believe that it is both possible and desirable for persons from diverse cultural backgrounds to maintain their cultural heritage and also to contribute positively and successfully to the dominant culture. This viewpoint is called cultural pluralism, and it is from the perspective of cultural pluralism that these biographies are written. They represent persons who identify strongly with their Hispanic heritage and at the same time who are proud of being citizens of the United States and successful contributors to U.S. society.

The biographies in these books represent the diversity of Hispanic heritage in the United States. Persons featured are contemporary figures whose national origins range from Argentina to Arizona and whose careers and contributions cover many aspects of contemporary life in the United States. These biographies include writers, musicians, actors, journalists, astronauts, businesspeople, judges, political activists, and politicians. Further, they include Hispanic women and men, and thus also characterize the changing role of all women in the United States. Each person profiled in this book is a positive role model, not only for persons of Hispanic heritage, but for any person.

Collectively, these biographies demonstrate the value of cultural pluralism and a view that the future strength of the United States lies in nurturing the diversity of its human potential, not in its uniformity.

Dr. Kathy Escamilla is currently Vice President of the National Association for Bilingual Education and an Associate Professor of Bilingual Education and Multicultural Education at the University of Colorado, Denver. She previously taught at the University of Arizona, and was the Director of Bilingual Education for the Tucson Unified School District in Tucson, Arizona. Dr. Escamilla earned a B.A. degree in Spanish and Literature from the University of Colorado in 1971. Her master's degree is in bilingual education from the University of Kansas, and she earned her doctorate in bilingual education from UCLA in 1987.

MAP OF THE WORLD

PACIFIC OCEAN

AUSTRALIA

ASIA

INDIAN OCEAN

EUROPE

AFRICA

SPAIN

GREENLAND

ATLANTIC OCEAN

DOMINICAN REPUBLIC

PUERTO RICO

CUBA

NORTH
AMERICA

CANADA

UNITED STATES

MEXICO

SOUTH
AMERICA

PACIFIC OCEAN

HAWAII

8

RAUL JULIA

Actor
1940–1994

"Raul loved his work," remembers his wife, Merel Poloway Julia. "He enjoyed becoming the character he would play on stage, in film, or on television. He was a very thoughtful man. He was funny and intelligent. He was never irrational. Once he made a decision, he was committed to it. No matter what he was doing, he was always happy. He was spontaneous and always a gentleman. **"**

Merel Julia, about her husband, Raul, as told to Barbara Marvis, February 1997

BIO HIGHLIGHTS

- Born March 9, 1940, in San Juan, Puerto Rico; mother: Olga Arcelay; father: Raul Julia
- Educated in Puerto Rico; attended the University of Puerto Rico where he earned a bachelor's degree in liberal arts
- Joined theater scene in San Juan; met Orson Bean who recommended he study acting in New York
- 1964, traveled to New York to study acting with Wyn Handman
- March 1964, first acting job in New York: *La vida es sueño (Life Is a Dream)*
- 1966, Joseph Papp hired Raul for the Spanish-language production of *Macbeth*
- 1967, starred as Conrad Birdie in Dallas production of *Bye Bye Birdie*
- 1968, made Broadway debut in *The Cuban Thing*
- 1970s, starred in film, television, and theater
- 1976, married Merel Poloway; son Raul Sigmund born in 1983; son Benjamin Rafael born in 1987
- 1980s, starred in *Kiss of the Spider Woman* and *The Tempest*
- 1990, starred in *Presumed Innocent* with Harrison Ford
- 1991, played Gomez Addams in *The Addams Family* and in its sequel in 1993, *Addams Family Values*
- Died October 24, 1994

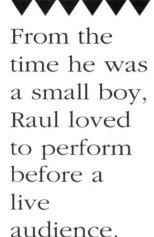

From the time he was a small boy, Raul loved to perform before a live audience.

RAUL JULIA

Raul Julia discovered he had a talent for acting when he was only five years old. He attended a Catholic elementary school, and the school play that year had a religious theme. First-grader Raul landed his first part on stage. He was going to play the devil. He took his assignment very seriously, learning all his lines. His great-aunt made him a beautiful costume. On the day of the play, Raul threw himself around on the stage. "I went crazy," he said later. His mother and some other parents thought he was having a fit. But soon it became clear that Raul was in complete control. He played his part perfectly—to the great relief of his mother and the nuns. Raul loved that first experience on stage. He loved to perform before a live audience. This first experience led Raul to a lifetime career as one of the most versatile performers on and off Broadway, on television, and in films.

Raul Rafael Carlos Julia y Arcelay was born on March 9, 1940, in San Juan, Puerto Rico. He was the oldest child of Raul Julia and Olga Arcelay. He had two sisters, Olga Maria and Maria Eugenia, and a brother, Rafael.

Raul's father held a degree in engineering from Tri-State University in Indiana. He worked for a while as an engineer, but later went into the restaurant business. He owned La Cueva del Chicken Inn, which he decorated to look like a Spanish gypsy cave. He served Spanish food, chicken-in-a-basket, and pizza. In the years after World War II, pizza had become very popular, and Raul's father was the first to introduce pizza in Puerto Rico.

Raul's mother, Olga Arcelay, was an amateur singer. She sang at church and at amateur operas. Raul remembered that when he was growing up, there was always music around. He said that things in his house tended to be humorous, musical, and dramatic—the perfect atmosphere for an aspiring actor.

Though his family spoke only Spanish at home, Raul was exposed to English at an early age. He attended a grade school in San Juan that was run by American nuns who spoke English a great deal of the time. From his earliest days, Raul enjoyed being the class clown.

Raul (front) with his mother, father, and brother, Rafael

RAUL JULIA

He loved to make his classmates laugh. "As a child, I thought theater was a school thing," he said later. "Something for people to come and see and laugh at. I never thought of it as a way of making a living." Raul had a part in the class play every year throughout grade school.

At San Ignacio de Loyola High School in San Juan, which Raul attended, the literature teachers taught Shakespeare by directing classroom performances of Shakespeare's plays. Raul was able to hear Shakespeare's language and to practice the dialogue throughout his high school years. This early training is what enabled him to become one of the best-known Shakespearean actors later in life.

After he graduated from high school, Raul attended the University of Puerto Rico. His parents wanted him to become a lawyer, so he studied psychology and law. But he was not happy. He switched departments and majors all through college until he admitted to himself that he really wanted to be an actor. Though his parents initially were not happy about his decision, they did eventually support him while he got his start. Raul earned a bachelor's degree in liberal arts and then set out to involve himself in the theater scene around San Juan. He found work with several local theatrical troupes. One of his first performances was in

▼▼▼▼▼▼

"I thought theater was a school thing," said Raul. "I never thought of it as a way of making a living."

▲▲▲▲▲▲

RAUL JULIA

Macbeth, which was performed outdoors in a sixteenth-century Spanish fort. He also worked at local nightclubs, and it was there that he caught the attention of Orson Bean, an American comedian. Mr. Bean thought Raul had great potential, and he advised him to go to New York City and study acting with Wyn Handman, an acting coach and the artistic director of the American Place Theatre. In 1964, at 24 years old, Raul decided to leave Puerto Rico for the United States. Before he left, however, his only brother, Rafael, was killed in a car accident. Though Raul was devastated, he left shortly thereafter for New York.

Raul's graduation photo from San Ignacio de Loyola High School in San Juan, Puerto Rico

RAUL JULIA

On the day that Raul arrived in New York City, it snowed. He had never seen snow before, because Puerto Rico's climate is subtropical. It marked the beginning of a new life.

Raul with his mother and two sisters, Olga Maria and Maria Eugenia

In March 1964, just a few weeks after he arrived, Raul found an acting job. He was cast in a play called *La vida es sueño* (*Life Is a Dream*), being performed in both English and Spanish at New York's Astor Theater. Raul played in the Spanish production. Though this job paid very little, he was able to apply for an Actors Equity card, which designated him as a professional actor. Many jobs are open only to Actors Equity members, and this was an important beginning for Raul.

Many acting jobs do not pay enough to cover ordinary living expenses. While an actor is trying to earn a name for himself, he often has to find additional means of support. Many actors become waiters, bartenders, and taxi drivers—jobs with flexible hours so that the actors can remain free for auditions. When Raul first arrived in New York, his parents sent him money to help with his expenses. As soon as he found work in his first play, he told his parents he no longer needed their help. Though his declaration of independence was a bit premature, Raul wanted to be able to make it on his own.

When Raul first went to New York City, he shared a tiny one-room apartment with another hopeful actor from Puerto Rico. "There were many hard times," he remembered. Raul took a job as a salesman, he tried to sell magazine subscriptions over the phone, and he gave Spanish lessons. No matter what he did, he was always very poor.

In the meantime, Raul followed Orson Bean's advice and took acting lessons from Wyn Handman. He also began to learn his

▼▼▼▼▼

When Raul first went to New York City, he shared a tiny one-room apartment with another hopeful actor from Puerto Rico.

▲▲▲▲▲▲

▼▼▼▼▼

It took Raul two years in New York to get his first break.

▲▲▲▲▲▲

way around Manhattan's theater district. At first, he did not have the experience to go to Broadway. And although there are many off-Broadway theaters as well, he could not get a part in an off-Broadway production, either. Many beginning actors would perform plays right on the street. Members of the Theater in the Street would bring plays to people who ordinarily could not afford to go to the theater. The actors benefited by getting additional practice and experience, and the audiences benefited by being exposed to the arts.

Raul gained much experience performing in the streets. But it was a dangerous profession. Many times, if the audience did not like an actor or part in the play, they would throw things onto the stage. Once, Raul was hit by an egg and a mattress. "If you can play in the street, you can play anywhere," Raul said years later. But Raul loved what he was doing, even though it was a tough way to start a career.

It took Raul two years in New York to get his first break. In 1966, Joseph Papp, founder of the New York Shakespeare Festival, produced a Spanish-language production of *Macbeth* to tour the city in a mobile stage unit. They gave performances in city parks for the growing Hispanic population. Raul landed the part of Macduff, a Scottish knight. Papp immediately recognized Raul's talent, and the two men became friends. Their friendship lasted for many years. Soon after *Macbeth,* Papp invited Raul to try out for a part in his next production, *Titus Andronicus.* Raul was cast as Demetrius. It was the first of many plays in which Raul would appear in Delacorte Theater in Central Park as part of the New York Shakespeare Festival.

Up until this time, Raul's acting parts relied on his Hispanic heritage. But in 1967, Raul went to Dallas to play Conrad Birdie, a teen idol, in the musical comedy *Bye Bye Birdie.* The play was about an Elvis Presley-like character, a popular American singer who had to enter the army. The producers were looking for a good-looking young man to play Conrad Birdie. Raul was tall, dark, and good-looking. He had no trouble looking the part of a teen idol. The play also required that he sing—something he had done all his life. In Puerto Rico, Raul had sung with a group called The Lamplighters.

After *Bye Bye Birdie,* Raul hit a dry spell where he could find no work. He called his friend Joseph Papp to see if he had anything. Papp hired Raul as his house manager until other acting parts appeared.

In September 1968, Raul finally had his Broadway debut. A short four years after he arrived in the United States, Raul won a part in *The Cuban Thing,* a play by Jack Gelber

▼▼▼▼▼▼
Joseph Papp recognized Raul's talent, and the two men became friends. Their friendship lasted for many years.
▲▲▲▲▲▲

RAUL JULIA

that dealt with Fidel Castro and the Cuban Revolution. Unfortunately, the play was not a success. It closed after thirteen previews and one performance. But Raul's performance was enough to bring him to the attention of important producers and directors, which led to many more parts.

Raul with Merel Poloway in 1972, several years before they were married

In the early 1970s, Raul met Merel Poloway, an actress and dancer with whom he had worked on several productions. Merel and Raul were married some years later, on June 28, 1976.

Though Raul's first passion had always been theater, he also became a success in film and television. In 1971, Raul received three minor parts in three movies: *The Organization,* a thriller about an organized drug-smuggling ring; *Been Down So Long It Looks Like Up to Me,* which starred Barry Primus and others, a film version of the book by Richard Farina about hip kids trying to endure life on a 1958 campus; and *The Panic in Needle Park,* a drama starring Al Pacino about a heroin shortage in New York City.

From these three films, Raul found that acting in front of a camera is very different from acting in front of a live audience. In the theater, the actor must do everything right the first time. The performance is live and people will see if the actor makes a mistake. Movies and television shows are usually taped. If the actor makes a mistake, the scene is shot again. Movie scenes are often not taped in the sequence in which they will appear but by the location of the scene. Theater provides immediate feedback to the actor about his performance. The actors can tell by the audience's reaction whether or not they have affected those watching. But in movies and television, the actors often have no live audiences, and, therefore, cannot assess their effect on an audience.

In the early 1970s, Raul also made his television debut. For a while, he held a regular part on the Children's Television Workshop show *Sesame Street.* He played the part of Rafael, who spoke Spanish. The producers at the time were making an effort to reach the Spanish-speaking children in the Puerto Rican districts of New York City. Raul also had a small part on a soap opera as a Cuban refugee.

▼▼▼▼▼
Raul found that acting in front of a camera is very different from acting in front of a live audience.
▲▲▲▲▲▲

RAUL JULIA

In 1971, Raul received his first Tony nomination for his portrayal of Proteus in *Two Gentlemen of Verona*. He was nominated a second time in 1974 for his performance in *Where's Charley?*, and a third time in 1976 for *Threepenny Opera*, where he played MacHeath. His fourth Tony nomination came in 1982 for *Nine*.

Raul starred with William Hurt (right) in *Kiss of the Spider Woman*.

In the 1980s, Raul appeared in many films, including *Compromising Positions*, *Tequila Sunrise*, and *Kiss of the Spider Woman*. In 1982, Raul came to the attention of the movie critics when he appeared as Kalibanos in Paul Mazursky's *The Tempest*.

Raul Julia

He worked with Mazursky again in 1988 in *Moon Over Parador*, for which he was nominated for a Golden Globe Award.

Though Raul Julia spent most of his life on stage and is well-known for his Shakespearean roles, he is perhaps most recognized by some of his last projects in the movies. In 1990, he starred in *Presumed Innocent* with Harrison Ford. This murder mystery cast Ford as an attorney who is accused of murder. Raul played Alejandro Stern, an attorney Harrison Ford's character hires to defend him. Then, in 1991, Raul starred as Gomez Addams in the movie *The Addams Family,* and in its sequel in 1993, *Addams Family Values*. The Addams family

Raul is perhaps best remembered for his comical portrayal of Gomez Addams in the movie *The Addams Family* and its sequel. Here he engineers a collision of his toy trains.

RAUL JULIA

had come to television in a series that had run from 1964 to 1966. "Raul was born to play Gomez," said director Barry Sonnenfeld. Raul enjoyed his zany roles, which reminded him of his childhood plays where he loved to make his audiences laugh.

Tragically, Raul Julia died from a stroke on October 24, 1994. He was only 54 years old. His family buried him in his homeland of Puerto Rico. His sons were only eleven and seven at the time of his death. His wife, Merel, provided us with some insight into her husband's life.

In addition to his love of acting, Raul was a devoted husband and father who adored his children. He and Merel had two sons, Raul Sigmund, born June 20, 1983, and Benjamin Rafael, born June 9, 1987. Though Raul had to travel and be away from his family a lot because of his career, he often brought the family on location with him. They visited many of his movie sets. Merel says that the family had to deal with his traveling, but they were together quite a bit. The family visited Yugoslavia, Brazil, and Argentina, locations where Raul was performing. They even watched Raul go hang gliding when they were in Brazil. When he was home, the family was always together. Though their main home is in New York City, they also own a home in the Catskill Mountains. It is beautiful country, and the

The Addams Family reminded Raul of his childhood plays where he loved to make his audiences laugh.

family has enjoyed riding horses there and getting away from city life.

"Raul loved his work," remembers Merel. "He enjoyed becoming the character he would play on stage, in film, or on television. He was a very thoughtful man. He

Raul with wife, Merel, and sons Raul Sigmund (right front) and Benjamin Rafael

RAUL JULIA

was funny and intelligent. He was never irrational. Once he made a decision, he was committed to it. No matter what it was he was doing, he was always happy. He was spontaneous, and always a gentleman.

"Raul was also a very caring person. In our travels, we saw a lot of poverty. He dedicated a great part of himself to ending hunger in the world. He educated himself about world hunger and was determined to conquer it in his lifetime. He saw ending hunger as his responsibility and he became a spokesperson on the subject. It didn't de-

From left to right: Actress Valerie Harper, Raul, and singer John Denver look at Ending Hunger picturebook at the Capitol on September 18, 1985. They introduced the book to the U.S. Senate.

crease his ability to live a joyful life, but he was determined to help. He was invited to speak all around the world. When he died, the Hunger Project created the Raul Julia Ending Hunger Project in his honor." Merel is the chairperson of that fund and she has committed one million dollars in her husband's name. In the first fiscal year, she raised $400,000, much of which benefited Latin American countries.

In September 1995, Raul was posthumously awarded the Hispanic Heritage Award for perpetuating a positive image of Hispanic culture and life. He has received many other honors since his death, including being inducted into the Theatre Hall of Fame at the Uris Theatre on Broadway in New York City.

To youngsters who would like to pursue an acting career, Merel feels that Raul would have this advice: "You don't need any advice. This is something you know inside yourself. Go after your heart's desire. That's what Raul did."

▼▼▼▼▼
Raul saw ending hunger as his responsibility and he became a spokesperson on the subject.
▲▲▲▲▲▲

MARIAH CAREY

Recording Artist, Songwriter, Producer
1970–

66 **W**hen I have a minute to reflect, I realize that my life has been pretty
amazing. But I consider myself a normal person who wants a normal life. It's exciting to
do what I do, but I also like to stay real and
grounded. **99**

Mariah Carey, as told to Alan W. Petrucelli of the *New York Post*

BIO HIGHLIGHTS

- Born March 27, 1970, on Long Island, New York; mother: Patricia Hickey Carey; father: Alfred Roy Carey
- Her parents divorced when she was two; her mother raised her alone
- In 1974, her mother, a professional singer and voice teacher, began giving her singing lessons
- For her sixteenth birthday, her brother gave her money to make a professional demo tape; met her first collaborator, Ben Margulies
- Graduated from Harborfields High School on Long Island in 1987
- Became a backup singer for Brenda K. Starr
- Landed a recording contract with CBS Columbia after handing a demo tape to record executive Tommy Mottola
- 1990, released her debut album, *Mariah Carey,* which won two Grammy Awards—best female pop vocal performance and best new artist
- Released second album, *Emotions,* in 1991, which she also produced, followed by third album, *MTV Unplugged EP,* in 1992
- Married Tommy Mottola on June 5, 1993, in New York City
- Released fourth album, *Music Box,* in August 1993 and fifth, *Merry Christmas,* in November 1994
- Released sixth album, *Daydream,* in 1995
- Started her own record label, Crave, in 1997
- Separated from Tommy Mottola in 1997

Mariah has
earned her
position as
a top
recording
artist
through her
own
merits—her
powerful
voice and
hard work.

Mariah Carey

In the Cinderella fairy tale, a poor unknown girl who is truly talented and beautiful meets a prince, whom she marries, and they live happily ever after. As a struggling New York singer, Mariah Carey's story has all the elements of the Cinderella story, except that her "prince" turned out to be a record producer. Far from finding accidental fame, she has earned her position as a top recording artist through her own merits—her powerful voice and hard work. The pop diva has even said, in describing her rags-to-riches career, "It really is like Cinderella."

But in this modern version of the story, instead of riding off in a silver coach and allowing herself to be waited on for the rest of her life, this hardworking Cinderella continues to challenge herself to perform ever more difficult jobs, from singer to composer to record producer.

Along the twists and turns of her life, Mariah has had her share of lucky breaks, but it has always been her talent and work ethic that have carried her through. She is the biggest-selling female vocalist of the 1990s. She has a breathtaking five-octave vocal range and a talent for writing and producing highly popular songs. Between 1990 and late 1996, she sold more than 80 million albums worldwide. She released 11 number-one pop singles, 5 number-one R&B

singles, and 3 number-one albums, and she received numerous awards, including two Grammy Awards.

Mariah Carey was born March 27, 1970, on Long Island, New York. She has no middle name. Her first name comes from the song "They Call the Wind Mariah," from the musical *Paint Your Wagon*. Mariah was the third of three children born to an opera singer mother, Patricia Hickey Carey, and an aeronautical engineer father, Alfred Roy Carey. Patricia had been raised in the Midwest by immigrants from County Cork, Ireland. Alfred, on the other hand, was of African-American and Venezuelan descent.

From the beginning of their marriage, in 1960, Patricia and Alfred felt the sting of prejudice due to their interracial union. Indeed, Mariah, as a mixture of several races, has had to endure various forms of racism from different ethnic groups throughout her life.

The first form of ostracism was from Patricia's parents and family, who disapproved of her marriage to Alfred. Patricia and Alfred had their first two children, a son, Morgan, in 1961, and a daughter, Alison, in 1962. The family moved from one all-white suburb to another on Long Island, enduring various forms of harassment. Before Mariah was even born, the discrimination the family suffered in the '60s—an era when

▼▼▼▼▼
Mariah, as a mixture of several races, has had to endure various forms of racism throughout her life.
▲▲▲▲▲▲

Mariah has been critcized for not embracing one particular ethnic group as her own. She prefers to be a part of all of them.

interracial marriages were not very common—was putting a strain on the relationship. Mariah told *People* magazine, "They went through some very hard times before I was born. They had their dogs poisoned, their cars set on fire and blown up." It put such pressure on them, said Mariah, "there was always this tension. They fought all the time."

All three of the children found themselves on the receiving end of prejudice. Alison, who was darker-skinned than the other children, was the brunt of taunts. The neighborhood kids would "shout racial slurs and beat her up," Mariah said, with a mixture of anger and sadness. "Then my brother would go in and fight for her even though he was handicapped [Morgan suffers from cerebral palsy and epilepsy]. It was tough."

Mariah experienced firsthand the trials of being an interracial child. She has been condemned at different times in her life for not coming out and embracing any particular ethnic group as her own, but she prefers to be part of all of them. She lived for a time with her African-American grandmother, which served to make her aware of her African-American heritage. And she certainly has shown a preference for soul, rhythm and blues, rap, and other African music types in her own singing career. But, she told a writer for *Ebony* magazine, "I always felt different from everyone else in my neighborhoods. I was a different person ethnically. And sometimes that can be a problem. If you look a certain way, everybody goes, 'White girl,' and I'd go, 'No, that's not what I am.'" Choosing to call herself black would have completely ignored her Irish mother, whom she calls her best friend. Saying she was black, Venezuelan, and Irish satisfied no one. So, she defined and continues to define herself as neither one group nor the other: "I am a human being, a person."

The marriage between Mariah's parents lasted only until Mariah was two years old. Patricia and Alfred divorced in 1972. Mariah's sister, Alison, chose to live with her father, and her brother, Morgan, left home shortly thereafter for college. As a result, Mariah was raised almost like an only child by her mother, who worked as a singer and freelance voice coach.

Mariah emulated her mother, a professional operatic mezzo soprano, and sang all the time while she was a young child playing in the house. Her amazing talent at mimicking sound was obvious from an early age. Mariah's mother told Steve Dougherty of *People* magazine in 1993, "From the time Mariah was a tiny girl, she sang on true pitch; she was able to hear a sound and duplicate it exactly." While rehearsing for her

▼▼▼▼▼
Mariah sang all the time while she was a young child playing in the house.
▲▲▲▲▲

MARIAH CAREY

New York City Opera debut in *Rigoletto,* Patricia missed her cue, but little Mariah chimed right in: "She sang it—in Italian—at exactly the right point. She wasn't yet three."

Impressed by her daughter's talents, in 1974, her mother began giving her singing lessons. But, according to Mariah, Patricia never pushed opera on her daughter. She let her go her own way, at the same time giving her a classical foundation that would help in the future. Mariah told *USA Today,* "She [Patricia] never said, 'Give it more of an operatic feel.' I respect opera like crazy, but it didn't influence me."

Mariah's influences were popular music she heard on the radio, which often served as her baby-sitter when she was growing up. She also liked the gospel music of Edwin Hawkins, the Clark Sisters, and Shirley Caesar, and the soul music of Gladys Knight, Stevie Wonder, Al Green, and Aretha Franklin. Every now and then she would listen to her mother's old records, fascinated by the stylings of Billie Holiday and Sarah Vaughan.

Mariah began writing poetry early, and these efforts would form a basis for writing lyrics. She began writing songs and lyrics in junior high. In high school, Mariah kept a low profile. A shy girl, she deliberately avoided showcasing her talent. She avoided the school choir and talent shows. Most of

Mariah began writing songs when she was in junior high school.

her classmates remember her as a normal student. While her music was still a personal, private endeavor, she was popular and was given the nicknames "Miss Mod" for her self-confident manner and "Mirage" for her frequent absences from class.

Remembering high school, she told Chris Nickson in a biography of her called *Mariah Carey: Her Story* (St. Martin's, 1995), "I'd hang out with my friends and go to parties, and just be stupid and goof off, but when I was at home, I was listening to music and writing songs." She developed a private, creative life at home that few of her friends witnessed. She completely focused on music. She told Nickson, "Girls growing up talk constantly about having babies. I talked about music."

While growing up, Mariah felt her friends didn't truly understand what it was like coming from a racially mixed background. She and Patricia lived on very little, and being raised by a single mother gave Mariah a sense of strength but also a certain amount of insecurity. She told Steve Dougherty of *People,* "I always felt like the rug could be pulled out from under me at any time. And coming from a racially mixed background, I always felt like I didn't fit [in] anywhere." Mariah spent her time and energy practicing her music rather than concentrating on getting good grades in

▼▼▼▼▼
She spent her time and energy practicing her music rather than concentrating on getting good grades in school.
▲▲▲▲▲▲

Mariah Carey

school. Several of her teachers tried to get her to focus more on her studies, but Mariah lived and breathed music. Despite her inattentiveness to her classes, she earned her diploma from Harborfields High School on Long Island in 1987.

During the end of her high school years, Mariah began a collaborating partnership with composer Ben Margulies. For her sixteenth birthday, her brother, Morgan, gave her the money to make a professional demo tape. She arranged to meet in a studio with a keyboardist, but he couldn't come, and by accident she stumbled upon Ben. Ben's father owned a cabinet factory in the Chelsea area of Manhattan, and he had allowed his son to set up a studio in a back room. Ben and Mariah wrote enough songs to create a demo tape.

After graduation, Mariah moved to New York City to pursue her career in earnest. She shared a one-bedroom apartment with two other girls who dreamed of becoming performers. She took a series of low-paying jobs—waitress, hatcheck girl, restaurant hostess, hair salon assistant—in order to finance her dream. When she wasn't working, she walked around to every record company in town, trying to get them to listen to her demo tape. After a few months, she auditioned and became a

For her sixteenth birthday, her brother, Morgan, gave her the money to make a professional demo tape.

backup vocalist for Brenda K. Starr, a pop artist who had a contract with Columbia Records.

Mariah's "discovery"—her break into the big time—happened in November 1988 after she reluctantly went to a record company party with Brenda K. Starr (to this day, Mariah avoids parties because she believes the cigarette smoke is bad for her voice). While at this particular party, she gave a demo tape to a dark, handsome man who, someone told her, was a Sony record executive. The man was Tommy Mottola, president of Sony Music Entertainment, parent company of Columbia Records.

At the time, Sony and Columbia were looking for a clear-voiced pop diva to compete with Whitney Houston, who was recording hits for a competitor. After leaving the party, Mottola listened to Mariah's tape in his car and became so excited about her voice that he asked his driver to turn his limousine around. He went back to the party to try to find her. But Mariah had already left. (For Mariah, in this part of her Cinderella story, the demo tape was her glass slipper!) It wasn't hard to locate Mariah the next day, though. Mottola told Fred Goodman of the *New York Times* in 1991, "When I heard and saw Mariah, there was absolutely no doubt she was in every way destined for stardom."

▼▼▼▼▼
At a party, Mariah gave her demo tape to Tommy Mottola, president of Sony Music Entertainment.
▲▲▲▲▲

MARIAH CAREY

Mariah immediately signed with Sony and set to work recording her first album, which contained polished songs written by other composers, designed to showcase her

Mariah displays her two Grammy Awards for best female pop vocal performance and best new artist.

smooth, five-octave voice. In 1990, Sony released her debut album, *Mariah Carey,* and presented their new talent to the world with music videos. Mariah Carey shot to number one on the Billboard chart and won two Grammy Awards that year—for best female pop vocal performance and best new artist. The public loved Mariah's voice, but some critics said the songs were too syrupy and light. In response to this, Mariah said, "A lot of people are singing about how screwed up the world is, and I don't think that everybody wants to hear about that all the time." Her fans love her for that optimism, as well as for her love songs and her fun-loving dance numbers.

What she could also have said, in her own defense, is that she wasn't the producer of the songs on her first album—they were handled by record-company crafters. On her successive albums, however, Mariah was able to showcase not only more of her songwriting and collaborating, but also her abilities as a producer. Unlike other pop stars, such as Whitney Houston and Madonna, Mariah writes and produces most of her own songs.

Despite the spotty reactions to her first album from music critics, all were impressed with Mariah's instrument—her voice. As Hillel Italie described it in the *Chicago Tribune,* "This is a voice that can probably shat-

▼▼▼▼▼▼
Mariah writes and produces most of her own songs.
▲▲▲▲▲▲

▼▼▼▼▼

On June 5, 1993, Mariah married Tommy Mottola, the man who discovered her talent.

▲▲▲▲▲▲

ter glass and then put it back together, that sounds as if she's taking the words and twirling them over her head like a cowboy with a lasso." David Smith of *Newsweek* described her voice as overwhelming: ". . . all seven or so octaves of it [he's deliberately exaggerating], from purring alto to stratospheric shriek. Up in this dog-whistle register, she can shape a scream into precise, synthesizer-like phrases. She has the good taste not to overuse this device, but how could anyone—especially a twenty-year-old—resist showing off just a little."

For her second album, released in 1991, Mariah was allowed to have more active involvement in production. The album, for which Mariah wrote all the lyrics, had a '70s R&B feel, so she dubbed it *Emotions* in honor of a female Motown group. *Emotions,* which made it to number four on the Billboard album chart, was followed by a studio session extended-play album created in conjunction with Mariah's appearance on MTV. *MTV Unplugged EP* was released in 1992 and peaked at number three on the Billboard album chart.

On Saturday, June 5, 1993, Mariah married Tommy Mottola in a storybook wedding in New York City. She wore a gown similar to that worn by England's Princess Diana in her royal wedding to Prince Charles. The megastar had come a long way

MARIAH CAREY

MARIAH CAREY

from the days when she had only one pair of tennis shoes and was running around New York dropping off demo tapes.

With Mariah in her gorgeous gown with a train so long it took six "ladies-in-waiting" to bring it into the church, it looked like the happy ending of the Cinderella story. But for Mariah, it was just the beginning. Getting married didn't slow her down at all. She was still keeping up her phenomenal pace of an album a year. Mariah released her fourth album, *Music Box,* in August 1993, and her fifth, *Merry Christmas,* in November 1994. For the first half of the '90s, her record-a-year total added up: *Mariah Carey* in 1990, *Emotions* in 1991, *MTV Unplugged EP* in 1992, *Music Box* in 1993, *Merry Christmas* in 1994, and *Daydream* in 1995.

In 1994, Mariah became a lifetime spokesperson for the Fresh Air Fund and committed $1 million to support a career awareness camp. "Camp Mariah" is named in honor of Mariah's dedication, support, and commitment to the disadvantaged young people who benefit from the program. The camp program raises money to help New York City children ages 12 to 15 explore different education and career options while taking part in summer camp adventures, as well as year-round activities in New York City, such as job shadowings,

▼▼▼▼▼

From 1990 until 1995, Mariah released an album each year.

▲▲▲▲▲▲

a career fair, and theme weekends focusing on such subjects as how to start your own business. Mariah is a popular spokesperson for the program. She has visited the camp several times and even took part in a foot-race with some of the kids.

Mariah's favorite colors, pink and black, are often reflected in her wardrobe. Her hobbies include swimming, horseback riding, waterskiing, and roller coaster riding. She loves animals. Besides her horses, she has four dogs: Jack, a Jack Russell terrier; Ginger, a Yorkshire terrier; and Duke and Princess, a pair of Dobermans. She also owns two Persian cats called

Mariah and husband Tommy attended a benefit for the Fresh Air Fund on June 6, 1996.

MARIAH CAREY

Tompkins and Ninja. More than anything, she likes to have what she calls a "normal" life. "When I have a minute to reflect," Mariah told Alan W. Petrucelli of the *New York Post,* "I realize that my life has been pretty amazing. But I consider myself a normal person who wants a normal life. It's exciting to do what I do, but I also like to stay real and grounded."

The best measure of Mariah's popularity is how much in demand she is from fans—reflected in record sales, MTV playing time, fan clubs, and Internet sites. Mariah's first four albums have sold a total of more than 16 million in the United States alone, and she has branched out to Europe and the Pacific Rim nations. As of late 1996, her first six albums had sold in excess of 80 million copies. Her first five singles all reached number one on the Billboard Hot 100 chart, a feat never accomplished before by any other artist—not even Elvis Presley or the Beatles. Music videos are a measure of success for modern recording artists, and Mariah shines there as well. Since her debut, she has consistently had at least two videos in the yearly Top 100 Video Countdown. She directs many of her videos.

While she didn't release an album in 1996, she had other projects in the works. She appeared as a guest artist on several other artists' albums, including the notorious

▼▼▼▼▼
As of late 1996, Mariah's albums had sold in excess of 80 million copies.
▲▲▲▲▲▲

MARIAH CAREY

B.I.G. and pop vocalists Boyz II Men. But an even bigger project—going up the next step in her career ladder—meant becoming a record producer, not of her own records,

Mariah sang on stage during the 23rd annual American Music Awards, January 1996.

MARIAH CAREY

Mariah sang at the
National Peace
Officers Memorial Day
Service in 1996.

Mariah sang at the National Peace Officers Memorial Day Service in 1996.

but of others'. In February 1997, a new record label was announced, with Mariah at the helm. Crave, a new Sony Music Independent Labels record company founded by Mariah, is a free-standing label. "I have watched and admired Mariah Carey's achievements as she has risen to become the most successful female singer of the 1990s," commented David Glew, president of Sony Music Independent Labels in a company press release. "She has successfully written and produced songs, for herself and others, so to bring these and other abilities to bear as the creative force behind a record label is a natural progression for her."

MARIAH CAREY

Mariah added: "Our main goal is to have a close-knit label where artists can feel comfortable, where we can discover some great music and get it the attention it deserves. As an artist and producer, I understand the need for creative freedom and how important that is to the process of making music. Letting artists be themselves and getting their music out to people—that's what Crave is all about."

In a nod to her own humble beginnings, Mariah's label will support new, struggling artists. Crave will support a diverse group, covering a wide spectrum of genres and music with global appeal. The label's first signing is a new female vocal group, Allure, whose first single is "Head Over Heels."

What's next for Mariah? Though she and her husband separated in early 1997, her career won't change much. She's certain to keep recording and producing for years to come and she may continue branching into other musical genres and stretching her range. She has recorded pop ballads and rap mixes; perhaps she'll venture into her classical training or experiment more with the Hispanic side of her heritage. She's proven she's no flash in the pan, and she has a bright future in front of her. "I don't want to be a 'big star,'" Mariah told *Ebony,* "but I want to be respected as an artist . . . this is

"Letting artists be themselves and getting their music out to the people— that's what Crave is all about."

"I want
to be
respected as
an artist. I
want to sing
for the rest
of my life."

▲▲▲▲▲▲

my love. I want to sing for the rest of my life."

It's no surprise that this kind of dedication is possible from a woman who knew she wanted to be a singer from the age of four. Mariah credits her mother for instilling confidence in her. While pondering the profession of singing, Mariah told Stephen Holden of the *New York Times,* "Because my mom did it for a living when I was young, I knew it could be more than a pipe dream. . . . My mom always told me, 'You are special. You have a talent.' She gave me the belief that I could do this."

DISCOGRAPHY

Selected Top Singles

"Vision of Love" (1990)

"Love Takes Time" (1990)

"Someday" (1991)

"I Don't Wanna Cry" (1991)

"Emotions" (1991)

"Can't Let Go" (1991)

"Make It Happen" (1992)

"I'll Be There" (1992)

"Dreamlover" (1993)

"Hero" (1993)

"Without You/Never Forget You" (1994)

"Anytime You Need a Friend" (1994)

"Endless Love" (1994) (duet with Luther Vandross)

"Fantasy" (1995)

"One Sweet Day" (1995)

"Open Arms" (1995)

"Always Be My Baby" (1995)

Albums

Mariah Carey (1990)

Emotions (1991)

MTV Unplugged EP (1992)

Music Box (1993)

Merry Christmas (1994)

Daydream (1995)

Video Collections

Mariah Carey—The First Vision (1991)

Mariah Carey—"MTV Unplugged" (1992)

Mariah Carey (1993)

Fantasy—Mariah Carey Live at Madison Square Garden

(1994)

48

ANDRES GALARRAGA

Professional Baseball Player
1961–

"**W**hen you have the opportunity to do what you love, put your heart into it. Dedicate yourself to it. Do it with love and much enthusiasm so that your dreams are realized. "

Andres Galarraga, as told to Tony Cantu, April 1997

BIO HIGHLIGHTS

- Born June 18, 1961, in Caracas, Venezuela; mother: Juana Galarraga; father: Francisco Padovani Galarraga
- January 19, 1979, Montreal Expos signed him as non-drafted free agent to play for their farm team
- 1984, married high school sweetheart, Eneyda Rodriguez
- 1985, called up to the Montreal Expos major-league team; named American Association's Rookie of the Year
- 1985, first daughter, Andria, was born in Caracas
- 1991, daughter Katherine born in Montreal
- 1991, injured his left kneecap; traded to the St. Louis Cardinals
- November 16, 1992, joined the Colorado Rockies
- 1993, won the National League Batting Title
- 1995, launched his own line of sports apparel and footwear

ANDRES GALARRAGA

When Andres Galarraga was growing up in Venezuela, he dreamed of being a baseball player. At the age of eight, he started playing as a first baseman for a team from his barrio, La Parroquia Chapellin, in Caracas, the capital of Venezuela. "We used to play barrio against barrio," he recalls. "I've loved baseball since I was very young. Ever since I was a child, I wanted to be a professional baseball player."

And so he continued to play and to watch his heroes—baseball legends Reggie Jackson and Roberto Clemente—on television. Although he was very far from the U.S. where his heroes played, he hoped that someday he would be among their ranks in the major leagues. He helped his team win several championships in Venezuela.

Today, Andres is one of the best players in major league baseball. He is the first baseman for the Colorado Rockies, an expansion team in the National League. He has won many baseball awards, including the National League Batting Title.

But getting to be one of baseball's best players was not easy. It took Andres many years of hard work and determination to achieve his dream.

Andres José Galarraga was born in Caracas, Venezuela, on June 18, 1961. The youngest of five children, he has three brothers and a sister. His father, Francisco, was a

▼▼▼▼▼
"Ever since I was a child, I wanted to be a professional baseball player."
▲▲▲▲▲▲

house painter in Venezuela, and his mother, Juana, is a housewife.

Though his family was not poor, baseball equipment was expensive, and not viewed as a necessity. It was not always easy to obtain the equipment Andres wanted. He recalls that his position in the family—the "baby" among the children—helped. "My brothers would help me out whenever I needed a glove, bat, ball, or uniform," he says. "We're a very united family. My parents always gave me support."

Although he played constantly, his family didn't realize how determined Andres really was. One of his brothers had played for a while, showing the same enthusiasm for the game as Andres, but then he quit playing. Andres, on the other hand, continued, getting better every year. Then, at the age of 18, Andres got his first chance to play in the United States. In January of 1979, the Montreal Expos signed him as a non-drafted free agent to play in their "farm system," on their minor-league team. The farm system was established to train young players for the major leagues. If a player shows he has grown enough in skill and experience, the team manager may "harvest" him from the farm team to play for the major-league team.

Being in the minor league does not guarantee a position in the majors. Some players spend their entire careers in the minor

▼▼▼▼▼

"My brothers would help me out whenever I needed a glove, bat, ball, or uniform."

▲▲▲▲▲▲

Andres Galarraga

leagues. Andres was willing to take that risk. Although he knew he'd miss his family, he also knew he had to follow his dream. "My family was in Venezuela, but I wanted to play baseball and I was given the opportunity," he recalls. "I didn't care about anything but playing."

His first assignment was to play on the minor-league team in West Palm Beach, Florida. He played just seven games there before being transferred to the A-ball team in Calgary, Alberta, Canada.

Although he started off slowly, Andres improved with each game. In his second year, his batting average was .263, up 49 points from his first year. By 1982, he had hit 14 home runs, connecting for double figures for the first time in his pro career. By this time, he was moved back to West Palm Beach, where he and his family maintain a home to this day.

In 1984, Andres was playing in Jacksonville, Florida, where he was voted as the Most Valuable Player (MVP) in the Southern

This photo was taken in 1990 when Andres played for the Montreal Expos.

League. His season average was .289, and he had hit 27 home runs.

Even with these successes, Andres was impatient. He wanted very badly to play in the major leagues. For some reason, the Montreal Expos were hesitant to call him up. "They wouldn't sign me because they said I was fat," Andres says. "They had seen me bat, but they had their doubts. They thought that I would gain weight."

At 6 feet 3 inches tall and fluctuating between 230 and 250 pounds, Andres is a large man. But he's not what you would call fat. In fact, even with his size, he is considered one of the most agile players in baseball. While playing in the minors, he earned the nickname The Big Cat, or *El Gato Grande* in Spanish, for his catlike reflexes and range at first base.

That's right—Andres was and is still playing first base, the position he has played since he was eight years old. "I've also played third base and outfield," Andres says. "But I like first base the best."

Not speaking any English and living far from his home, Andres says it was hard coming to the U.S.: "*Dificilisimo,*" he recalls. ("Very hard.") Although he was at that point married to a young woman he had met in school in Venezuela, he missed his country, he says. And, despite worries about his weight, he admits that he missed the meals

▼▼▼▼▼

While playing in the minor league, Andres earned the nickname The Big Cat, or *El Gato Grande* in Spanish, for his catlike reflexes and range at first base.

he used to get in Venezuela. "At first I felt different," he says. "I didn't speak any English. Everything was different and strange, including the food."

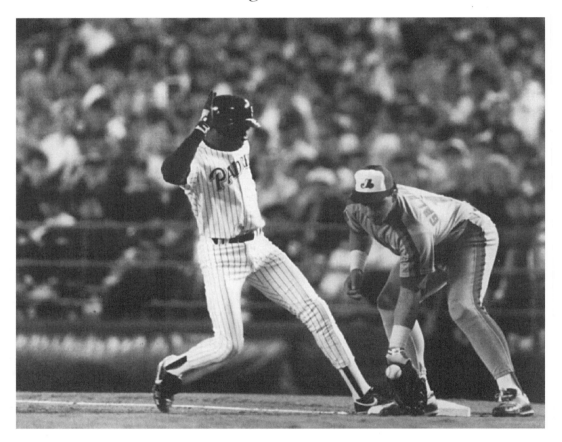

Tony Fernandez of the San Diego Padres returned to first base before Andres caught the ball in their pickoff attempt, July 23, 1991.

By 1985, Andres was moved yet again, to Indianapolis to play for the AAA-team for the Cincinnati Reds. He continued to play with enthusiasm. Later that year, after playing much of the season in Indianapolis, he got his big chance with the Montreal Expos.

ANDRES GALARRAGA

Finally, Andres was called up to the major leagues!

Andres was then 23 years old. He was extremely motivated his first year as a pro—so much so that he was named the American Association's Rookie of the Year. His batting average was .269, with 25 homeruns and 87 runs batted in (RBIs).

In Venezuela, his success was closely watched by his countrymen. Newspapers there, such as *El Diaro* (of Caracas) and *El Universal,* Venezuela's largest paper, often reported his achievements on the front page. On holidays and when baseball season was over, Andres would visit his relatives in Venezuela. His wife, Eneyda, also has family there. Their first daughter, Andria, was born in Caracas on December 27, 1985. (Their younger daughter, Katherine, was born in Montreal on August 16, 1991.) In 1987, sportswriters in Venezuela voted Andres athlete of the year. His wife and daughter read the news in *El Mundo,* a Spanish-language newspaper, when they were in their home in Florida. Andres was extremely happy. "I always dreamed of obtaining this honor, and my dreams have been fulfilled," he told *El Mundo.* "I'm a very happy man."

To this day, whenever Andres goes to Venezuela, he is mobbed. He is considered the Michael Jordan of Venezuela, the most popular athlete from that country. He is es-

▼▼▼▼▼ Newspapers in Venezuela often report Andres' achievements on the front page. Whenever he goes to Venezuela, he is mobbed. He is the most popular athlete from that country. ▲▲▲▲▲▲

ANDRES GALARRAGA

pecially admired by the young people there. Andres takes this role very seriously. With the endorsement of a beverage company,

46 Martes 15 de diciembre de 1987 EL DIARIO DE CARACAS

DEPORTES

Andrés Galarraga, el inicialista de Los Leones del Caracas en la pelota profesional venezolana y de los Expos de Montreal en el beisbol de grandes ligas, fue seleccionado como Atleta del Año, mención que otorga anualmente el Círculo de Periodistas Deportivos, que preside Abelardo Raidi.

Ayer se realizó una reunión en la sede del CPD para dar a conocer la votación para la selección del deportista más destacado en el año 1987. Participaron miembros de la junta directiva e integrantes de la entidad que aglutina a los periodistas deportivos.

De acuerdo al escrutinio final, resultó favorecido Galarraga con un total de 881 puntos seguido de Renzo Berto y de Antonio Esparragoza, quienes ocuparon el segundo y tercer lugar en forma respectiva. También recibieron votos e integran el grupo de los diez mejores atletas del año, Ricardo Jiménez, Omar Catarí, Baudilio Díaz, José Lindarte, Marietta Riera, María Carolina Rivera y Carlos Rivas.

Andrés Galarraga este año cumplió su segunda campaña como grande liga y fue su primera completa; culminó su actuación con un sobresaliente promedio de 305 puntos, además empujó 90 carreras y conectó 15 jonrones, quedando entre los diez mejores bateadores de la Liga Nacional.

Renzo Berto, el falconia-

Círculo de Periodistas Deportivos emitió veredicto

Andrés Galarraga fue seleccionado el mejor atleta del año 1987

Renzo Berto lo secundó en la votación y Antonio Esparragoza quedó de tercero. La Feve-Tiro fue escogida como la entidad deportiva del año y su presidente, Oscar Vivas Arellano, el dirigente del año

La directiva del CPD se reunió ayer para dar a conocer que Andrés Galarraga fue escogido Atleta del Año.

no que lo secundó en la votación para atleta del año 1987, se posesionó de la medalla de oro en el tiro de los Juegos Panamericanos de Indianápolis en la modalidad de fuego central individual. Antonio Esparragoza obtuvo el título mundial de la división pluma de la AMB al vencer a Steve Cruz y después defendió en forma exitosa la faja contra Pascual Aranda.

Ricardo Jiménez, quien quedó de cuarto en la votación, fue el mejor nadador de los pasados juegos nacionales juveniles de Maracay al conseguir nueve medallas y representó al país en los Panamericanos de Indianápolis.

Omar Catarí, otro peso pluma pero de renglón amateur, apareció en el quinto lugar gracias a las

medallas de oro logradas en el campeonato Centroamericano de Costa Rica, en la Copa Simón Bolívar de Barquisimeto y en el torneo Vásquez Raña de México.

Baudilio Díaz consiguió un excelente performance como receptor de los Rojos de Cincinnati, mientras que José Lindarte ganó la Vuelta a Venezuela en bicicleta; Marietta Riera fue medallista de bronce en el lanzamiento de la jabalina en los Panamericanos de Indianápolis y superó el record nacional.

Por su parte María Carolina Rivera fue la mejor atleta de los Nacionales Juveniles de Maracay al aduañarse de 11 medallas de oro en la natación y sumó otra de bronce. Terminó el cuadro de los diez mejores atletas del año Carlos Rivas, ganador de presea de oro en el Tae Kwoun Do (artes marciales) durante los Panamericanos de Indianápolis.

También en la reunión del CPD se dieron a conocer los ganadores en otros renglones. **Dirigente del año:** Oscar Vivas Arellano, presidente de Feve-Tiro que, por cierto, fue la entidad del año. **Entrenador del año:** Pedro "Camagüey" Espinoza (basket); empresa que más ayudó al deporte: Banco Construcción. Además, se decidió entregar un reconocimiento a la bolichera Daisy Torrevilla por su juego perfecto de 300 puntos este año. El 18 de enero se entregarán los premios.

MAA

El Diario of Caracas, Venezuela, often prints stories about Andres.

Andres visits schools and inspires young people. He even conducts baseball clinics in Venezuela, giving youngsters tips on their game. "I'm an example for the young people," Andres says proudly. "I'm the athlete they invoke for children to watch."

And, indeed, the young Venezuelans watch, drawing on Andres as an example of what can be achieved with hard work and determination. Andres does not disappoint them. In 1989, he hit his first grand slam home run. (A grand slam is a home run hit when all the bases are loaded.) That year, he also excelled at defense, which helped him earn his first Gold Glove, a prestigious award.

Galarraga belts 529-foot grand slam

Associated Press

MIAMI — Andres Galarraga hit a 529-foot grand slam Saturday, then was ejected four innings later for charging the mound after being hit by a pitch in the Colorado Rockies' 8-4 victory over the Florida Marlins.

Galarraga's slam against Kevin Brown was the longest home run ever at Pro Player Stadium, the longest in Rockies history and the longest this season in the major leagues.

Mickey Mantle is generally credited with hitting the longest home run ever, a 565-foot drive in 1953 off Washington's Chuck Stobbs at Griffith Stadium.

PADRES 12, ASTROS 5 — Wally Joyner and John Flaherty each drove in three runs, sending San Diego past Houston.

EXPOS 4, PIRATES 2— Rondell White and Darrin Fletcher homered in succession in the first inning, then singled to start a two-run fourth to lead Montreal past Pittsburgh.

CUBS 7, REDS 4— Shawon Dunston doubled twice, singled and drove in two runs as Chicago defeated Cincinnati.

CARDINALS 6, DODGERS 3 — Hot-hitting John Mabry went 3-for-4 with a two-run homer and St. Louis took advantage of some shaky Los Angeles fielding for the victory.

Todd Stottlemyre (4-3) allowed three runs and six hits in 8 1-3 innings as the Cardinals won for the sixth time in seven games. He had a season-high 10 strikeouts and walked two before being replaced by Dennis Eckersley, who got the final two outs for his 11th save.

The next year was almost a repeat of the previous one, as Andres hit his second grand slam in August, the same month he had hit the one in 1989. And he earned another Gold Glove Award for his performance in 1990.

Those were good years for Andres. He enjoyed being honored in the United States, but he was even more proud of the recognition he received in Venezuela.

Andres has hit several grand slams. This article tells about his 529-foot grand slam in June 1997.

"The negative things that have happened to me were really a help because they made me work harder and concentrate more. I like the challenge."

ANDRES GALARRAGA

However, his happiness was short-lived. Andres had been a favorite of the Montreal fans until 1991. In that year, his average fell to just .219, with nine homers in 107 games. In June of that year, he was unable to play because of an injury to his left kneecap. He was sidelined for 36 games. Thinking his best days were behind him, Montreal traded him for another player. After 13 years, Andres was no longer a member of the Montreal Expos.

Things got worse. He was traded to the St. Louis Cardinals, and after just one week of playing for his new team, his father died of cancer. Barely one month later, his aunt, who lived next door to his parents in Caracas, also died. Then, in the second game of the regular season, Andres was hit by a pitch that broke his right hand. He was unable to play for 44 games. When he returned, he was booed by the fans. Because he was recovering from his injury, and because of his mental state after the death of his father, Andres was not playing well. He was hitting so poorly that at one point the manager in St. Louis, Joe Torre, pinch hit for him, batting in his place. That caused Andres much embarrassment.

Today, Andres is philosophical about those dark days. "The negative things that have happened to me were really a help because they made me work harder and concentrate more," he says. "I like the challenge. When people say, 'You can't do that,' I think 'yes' and prove it. The negative comments have made me work harder and try to overcome and improve."

He applied that philosophy to improve his game for his new team. He sought the help of batting coach Don Baylor. Together they watched old films of Andres and decided he needed to change the way he batted. Andres used to bat with a closed stance, with his left foot much closer to home plate than his right. He then discovered his left eye was not as strong as his right, so he and Don decided that he should shift his head slightly so that he could directly face the pitcher.

After many sessions with Don, Andres started batting with his legs more spread out. In fact, the way he now stands at the plate is considered one of the most exaggerated open stances in baseball.

Andres stands at the plate with one of the most exaggerated open stances in baseball.

ANDRES GALARRAGA

It's a home run!

But it worked. In the second half of 1992, fully recovered from his hand injury, Andres became once again a powerful hitter. Before

his injury, Andres had a low batting average of .189, but after adopting his new batting stance, he hit .301 in the final 45 games, with 8 home runs and 29 RBIs.

Still, his poor performance earlier in the season prompted St. Louis to let him go. Andres was disappointed. Then Don Baylor, who had helped him so much during that horrible year, got a job as the manager of the Colorado Rockies. The Rockies were an expansion team, a team that had grown from an expanded major league. With his friend as manager there, Andres knew that that was the team he wanted to play for.

On November 16, 1992, Andres joined the Colorado Rockies. And the best was yet to come.

At first, the Rockies were not too sure how well Andres would do, so they gave him a contract for just one year at $600,000. But in 1993, Andres played with a vengeance. Don Baylor hoped Andres's batting average would be at least .270. Instead, Andres batted .370, the best of all the league players that year.

As a result, Andres won the National League Batting Title, one of the highest honors in the major leagues. He was the first Venezuelan and the first player from an expansion team ever to win the batting title. His average of .370 was the highest by a right-handed hitter in the majors since 1939,

▼▼▼▼▼

In 1993, Andres won the National League Batting Title. He was the first Venezuelan and the first player from an expansion team ever to win the title.
▲▲▲▲▲

ANDRES GALARRAGA

Andres loves to play baseball. He wants to help his team win every game.

when Joe DiMaggio hit .381. It was also the highest for a right-handed player in the National League since Joe "Ducky" Medwick hit .374 in 1937.

ANDRES GALARRAGA

Andres was also honored that year by being selected to play in the all-star game. He was the first representative from the Colorado Rockies to be picked for the game. At the time of the all-star break, Andres had an astounding batting average of .391.

Because of his performance, Andres's agent decided it was time to renegotiate his contract. After meeting with the team representatives, Andres emerged with a four-year salary of $17.5 million.

Despite his tremendous success, Andres has never forgotten his roots. He still prefers to speak in Spanish. And he insists that his daughters, who are bilingual, speak Spanish at home. "*Aqui se habla Español,*" he says. ("Here, Spanish is spoken.") "In school, they can speak their language, but at home . . ."

He remembers during his early years, when he was a struggling but enthusiastic player, that he was helped by other Latino players, some from other teams. When they talked to him in Spanish, he said it helped him get over his homesickness. He said he still enjoys that camaraderie.

In 1993, Andres played with a vengeance.

ANDRES GALARRAGA

"We have that in common, whether they're Mexican, Puerto Rican, or Dominican, from wherever," he says. "We even correct ourselves. At the time of the game, it's not that we're enemies, but we don't interact. But after the game, wherever we see each other, we are normal friends and tell each other, 'You're doing this wrong,' or 'You should do it this way.' Or if we did something right, we congratulate each other."

In 1995, Andres launched his own line of sports apparel and footwear, something that only the most famous athletes can do. He was prompted to do this partly because he wanted the children in Venezuela to be able to buy merchandise that had the name of their hero, *El Gato Grande,* emblazoned on it.

Andres still goes to Venezuela to visit his family every year. Sometimes, his family travels to the U.S. to see him play.

In 1997, he was 35, considered somewhat old in professional athletics, but he says he hopes to play until he is 40. The key to his success, he says, is that he plays every game with the same enthusiasm as when he was a child playing in Venezuela and dreaming of becoming a professional baseball player.

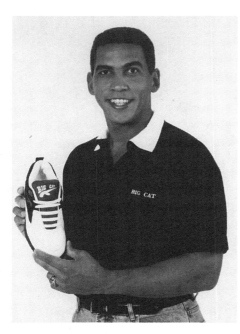

In 1995, Andres launched his own line of sports apparel and footwear. He wants the children of Venezuela to be able to purchase merchandise with the name of their hero, *El Gato Grande,* emblazoned on it.

ANDRES GALARRAGA

Recently, Andres played in an exhibition game in Japan. He got to play with other famous players, such as Cal Ripken Jr., Barry Bonds, Ken Griffey Jr., and Juan Gonzalez. "It was like another dream that presented itself," he says of the opportunity to play with those players.

The road from the barrios of Venezuela to the major leagues was not easy for Andres. But he offers this advice to young people who want to succeed in life: "First, study and do what you love or what you're best at. Second, when you have the opportunity to do what you love, put your heart into it. Dedicate yourself to it. Do it with love and much enthusiasm so that your dreams are realized."

Andres gives high fives to his teammates after winning a game in 1996.

MARY JOE FERNANDEZ

Professional Tennis Player
1971–

"Everybody's different, and everybody matures at a different time—mentally and physically. So it's hard to say at what age it's right or wrong for a person to turn pro. What I would say, though, is that you should finish school first, because there's always time to play tennis afterward, and an education balances out your life. As a professional athlete, you never know what's going to happen to you next week. . . . If you have your education, you've got something to fall back on.**"

Mary Joe Fernandez, as told to Lucy Danziger for *Interview*, June 1994

BIO HIGHLIGHTS

- Born Maria José Fernández on August 19, 1971, in the Dominican Republic; mother: Silvia Pino Fernández; father: José Fernández
- Showed an interest in and talent for tennis from the age of three
- Attended private Carrollton School of the Sacred Heart in Miami
- At ten, won the United States Tennis Association (USTA) Nationals for players 12 and under
- From age 11 to 14, won four consecutive singles age group titles at the Orange Bowl, the first girl to do so; in 1984, captured USTA championship for girls 16 and under
- Joined the Women's Tennis Association (WTA) professional ranks at the age of 14 and became youngest player to win a match in the U.S. Open
- Graduated from Carrollton in 1989
- 1992, won a gold medal with Gigi Fernandez in the Olympics at Barcelona, as well as a bronze in singles
- Won the Brighton International title in 1995
- Won gold medal in doubles, with Gigi Fernandez, in 1996 Olympics in Atlanta
- As of March 1997, had won six singles titles in major tournaments and thirteen doubles titles, including the Australian and European Opens

MARY JOE FERNANDEZ

When Mary Joe Fernandez was just three years old, she would tag along with her father, José, and her older sister, Mimi, when the two went to play a game of tennis. Like any toddler, Mary Joe wanted to mimic what her sister and father were doing, so José gave her a tennis racket to keep her occupied and out of harm's way. She was perfectly content to bounce balls off a wall, using a racket that her father had whittled down to fit her small hand. Two years later, at the age of five, she was taking tennis lessons from a professional player. It was the start of a career for Mary Joe.

The rather unusual name of Mary Joe is the Anglicized version of her real name, Maria José Fernández. When she was born on August 19, 1971, in the Dominican Republic, her parents gave her her father's name for a middle name.

Her father, José Fernández, came from Spain, and he met his future wife, Silvia Pino, in '50s Havana, Cuba, where she lived and he was visiting. They were married in Havana, but when Fidel Castro and his Revolutionary Army came to power and took over the Cuban government in 1959, José and Silvia and their extended family fled the country and settled in the Dominican Republic. Their first daughter, Silvia "Mimi" Fernández, was born there. Mary Joe was also born there. When Mary Joe was three months old, the family left the Dominican Republic to start a new life in the United States. They settled in Miami, Florida.

José Fernández is now an attorney who also owns a real estate firm in South America and who travels regularly on the Women's Tennis Association (WTA) Tour with Mary Joe. He doesn't actively coach her, but he stays involved with her training and tournament schedule. Her mother is a real estate broker in Florida. Mimi, with whom Mary Joe is very close, lives in Miami with her family, composed of husband Chris and daughters Megan and Carolina.

When José saw the way his three-year-old daughter took to the customized racket, he encouraged her to keep hitting balls. By the time she was five, he was convinced that she had a particular talent for the sport. He consulted a U.S. tennis champion, Gardner Mulloy, for advice. Mulloy came to watch Mary Joe, and he advised José to enter her in as many tournaments as possible.

The United States Tennis Association (USTA) hosts amateur tournaments for budding tennis players. Their lowest age bracket is "twelves," a category for players 12 years old and younger. Mary Joe won the USTA Nationals in the twelves bracket at the age of ten. After winning, Mary Joe was accused by envious parents of her opponents of being older than she claimed. These parents

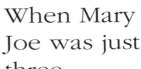

When Mary Joe was just three months old, her family left the Domincan Republic to start a new life in the U.S.

Mary Joe played in her first professional tournament when she was just 13 years old. She participated as an amateur.

made the unfounded suggestion that Mary Joe's parents had falsified her birth certificate before the family came to America. This petty rivalry was the family's first experience with the bigoted attitude toward foreigners sometimes found in U.S. sports.

Mary Joe soon quieted her detractors. From age 11 to 14, she won four consecutive singles USTA championship age-group titles at the Orange Bowl in her hometown of Miami. She was the first girl to win so many back-to-back titles. Even more remarkable, each time, she was younger than the age limit of the division in which she competed. At 11, she won the singles title for players 12 and under. In 1984, at the age of 13, she captured the title for girls 16 and under. And the next year, at age 14, she won the championship for girls 18 and under.

Her school friends remember that Mary Joe, recalled as a pretty, skinny, dark-skinned girl with long dark hair, was the type of person who never did anything wrong. They jokingly called her Miss Goody Two-shoes. One high school friend remembered an episode when she and Mary Joe were going to confession, and Mary Joe came to her in a panic, saying, "You've got to help me think up some sins!"

She played in her first professional tournament when she was 13, participating as an amateur. She beat her first-round op-

MARY JOE FERNANDEZ

MARY JOE FERNANDEZ

ponent, 33-year-old Pam Teeguarden, but lost the next match. That same year, she defeated the world's 11th-ranked player, Bonnie Gadusek.

As Mary Joe became a better and better player on the junior circuit, she made a big decision. With the support and encouragement of her family, she decided to turn professional at the age of 14. Turning pro meant earning money for tournament wins, but the decision brought with it a great deal of pressure. Agents, fellow players, and fans immediately began urging her to drop out of school, as many other young tennis stars do. But she announced instead that she would attend the private Catholic prep school, Carrollton School of the Sacred Heart, and play professional tennis on a part-time basis.

In taking the road less traveled, Mary Joe showed a great deal of resolve, and the decision was a testimony to her parents' support and her own self-motivation. In professional tennis, it is not uncommon for young players to drop out of school, study with a tutor, and focus full-time on tennis. Many players do this in the hope of earning more money, reaching their full potential at an earlier age, and having a longer tennis career. Yet sometimes following this path is bad for the person's development. More often than not, the players never finish their

With the support and encouragement of her family, Mary Joe turned professional at the age of 14.

studies and focus solely on the sport. Their parents—usually fathers—gain a bad reputation as "stage-door" parents, who push the children and are only interested in the money the children can make. "Tennis fathers" are a common occurrence, because, unlike other industries, the sport doesn't have any child labor laws, and when some parents figure out that their child can make much more money than they can, they push the child even harder. Players as different as Monica Seles, Mary Pierce, and Jennifer Capriati have, like Mary Joe, been propelled by their fathers, but with much different results.

Mary Joe and her father have always been close, and she says she never received this kind of pressure from him. The fact that she finished school is clear evidence of that. Even though she entered four Grand Slam tournaments and several others during a three-and-a-half-year period in high school, she worked those tournaments around her classes. "If Mary Joe doesn't want to study, we make her study," her father told *Sports Illustrated*. "If she doesn't want to play tennis, we don't make Mary Joe play."

When it came to staying in school and therefore staying close to her friends, Mary Joe was just as determined as her parents. Despite the continuing lure of more money and celebrity throughout her high school

▼▼▼▼▼▼
Mary Joe and her father have always been close.
▲▲▲▲▲▲

"I had a lot of pressure when I was 13 or 14 to drop out and dedicate myself fully to tennis. . . . You need an education to fall back on."

years, she knew that staying in school was the right choice. "I had a lot of pressure when I was thirteen or fourteen to drop out and dedicate myself fully to tennis. A lot of kids do that," Mary Joe told a reporter for *USA Weekend*. "But I finished high school. You don't know if you'll break a leg or get burned out. You need an education to fall back on."

Furthermore, after she made this decision, she stuck with it, trying her best to succeed in school. "I just decided that if I was going to go to school, I was going to do it right," she said. "And I wasn't ready to sacrifice being with my friends." She also explained, in the September 1991 issue of *Cosmopolitan,* her reasoning behind the decision to split her time between tennis and school: "I might have lost touch with reality. If you go to beautiful places all the time, as you do on the tennis tour, you think that's how it is everywhere."

It's a sad reality that many people in professional sports ignore their education, and women's tennis is one of the worst examples. In this sport, many do not have their high school diplomas. According to Michael Mewshaw in his book *Ladies of the Court: Grace and Disgrace on the Women's Tennis Tour* (Crown Publishers, 1993), too often people don't seem to care or notice that "tennis players received less formal education than any athletes in the world, with the possible exception of boxers or bullfighters."

Therefore, Mary Joe became known as "the one who finished school." When she was asked by Lucy Danziger of *Interview* magazine in 1994 what she thought about young kids turning pro, she responded: "Everybody's different, and everybody matures at a different time—mentally and physically. So it's hard to say at what age it's right or wrong for a person to turn pro. What I would say, though, is that you should finish school first, because there's always time to play tennis afterward, and an education balances out your life. As a professional athlete, you never know what's going to happen to you next week. . . . If you have your education, you've got something to fall back on."

All through high school, Mary Joe maintained an A average while earning more than $500,000 in tournament prize money. Sometimes, when she missed class due to a tournament, her friends, who called her May Jay, helped her out by faxing their class notes to her or dictating them to her over the telephone. They would sometimes be dismayed when Mary Joe would score higher on the tests than they did!

Her class graduated from Carrollton in 1989, but Mary Joe missed commencement ceremonies in order to play in the French

▼▼▼▼▼

Mary Joe graduated from high school in 1989, but she missed commencement ceremonies to play in the French Open.

▲▲▲▲▲

Mary Joe Fernandez

Open. She was allowed to take her senior class final exams in August rather than in June because of the tournament. Nevertheless, thanks to the help of her friends and her own hard work, she graduated with honors. In 1990, just a year after graduating, she represented the Women's Tennis Association (WTA) on the Players Council.

Soon after she turned pro in 1985, Mary Joe became the youngest player to win a match in the U.S. Open. But she won only one match. She was defeated in the second one by one of her tennis idols, Chris Evert. Mary Joe calls Evert her childhood hero: "When I was 13, 14, 15, I played Chris a lot. I never beat her. She never let me." Indeed, Mary Joe's competitive nature comes out when she is asked if she ever lets anyone beat her. She pooh-poohs the idea outright. In tennis, she says, "Fight your heart out, then leave it on the court."

Mary Joe is similar to Chris Evert in other ways. As a female and an athlete, it is important to her to appear feminine. A traditional, conservative young woman, Mary Joe puts forth a ladylike image that is lacking in some of the other players. "A woman should be feminine, on court and off," she told writer Michael Mewshaw. "I wouldn't like to look muscular or masculine. But in my opinion, if you're a woman, you should look like one." Perhaps it was these kinds

▼▼▼▼▼
Soon after she turned pro in 1985, Mary Joe became the youngest player to win a match in the U.S. Open.
▲▲▲▲▲▲

of comments that led Mewshaw to observe Mary Joe closely and to describe her in his book this way: "A mahogany-brown, imperially slim girl of nineteen, she had a cat's sinuous grace and slinky deceptive speed. Dark hair hung down her back in a single braid. Her sinewy legs were those of a dancer, her frail upper body that of a model." Mary Joe completes the picture by choosing to wear floral prints, keeping her hair long, and never yelling or grunting as some of her competitors do.

In her first full season as a professional, she won 40 of 50 singles matches, two tournaments, and more than $1 million in prize money and endorsements. She reached her first Grand Slam singles final in January 1990 at the Australian Open, but lost the title to Steffi Graf in a close match. By February she had made it into the top ten without having won a professional title. And she captured her first pro championship at the Tokyo Indoors in September 1990.

Getting to that first professional championship was extremely harrowing. In the Tokyo tournament, she won a three-hour come-from-behind match against Manuela Maleeva-Fragniere. But after the win—in an extremely hot indoor gym—her abdominal muscles had to be packed in ice because a visible knot was forming in one of her muscles. "We could hear her screaming,"

▼▼▼▼▼

In her first full season as a professional, Mary Joe won 40 of 50 singles matches.

▲▲▲▲▲▲

said her hitting partner, Dean Goldfine. "It was a little scary."

Mary Joe had never experienced such pain. A Japanese doctor relieved her agony by giving her herbal therapy and accupressure. Miraculously, the next day she got back on the court, feeling very stiff, and beat Amy Frazier for the title. She celebrated her first professional championship title by sleeping for 12 hours.

During the rest of that season, Mary Joe continued to suffer several kinds of injuries, and looking back, she believes it was because she wasn't in top condition because of the part-time schedule of her high school years. She was sidelined with a torn hamstring (in March 1990 at a Virginia Slims of Florida match against rival Gabriela Sabatini), a back injury (incurred during the third round of the German Open), a severe knee sprain (which occurred while training for Wimbledon and prevented her from competing successfully in that tournament), severe dehydration, and tendinitis in her right shoulder. In school, her classmates had teased her for not being able to pass the President's Council on Physical Fitness test because she couldn't hold the arm hang long enough. Some tennis observers speculated that her many injuries were the result of not following a consistent conditioning program. Others blamed the meat-grinder aspect of

▼▼▼▼▼

Mary Joe suffered several painful injuries early in her career.

▲▲▲▲▲▲

the women's tour or that her management was simply scheduling her in too many tournaments.

In *Ladies of the Court,* Michael Mewshaw describes a physically depleted player who was obviously suffering during the U.S. Open:

> Pale and gaunt, Mary Joe Fernandez arrived at Court Sixteen for her third-round match. . . . I wasn't prepared for how sickly she looked or how pathetically she played. Perspiration ran in rivulets down her arms and legs, soaking her shirt and even her skirt, leaving puddles on the court. . . . Mary Joe requested an injury time-out, and Kathleen Stroia, the WTA trainer, massaged her legs. Then she wrapped Mary Joe's left leg from the panty line down to the mid-thigh. A fan wolf-whistled, but it was doubtful Fernandez heard him or would have cared if she had. She was sunk too deep in her own misery. She played one game wearing the leg wrap, tore it off, promptly fell behind 2-5, and watched helpless as [Radka] Zrubakova

▼▼▼▼▼▼

Some blamed her management for scheduling her in too many tournaments.

▲▲▲▲▲▲

served out the match for a shocking 6-1, 6-2 win.

It would have been understandable if Mary Joe had skipped the press conference. But she dutifully endured it and refused to blame the loss on her physical debility. "I just had a flat day." She did admit to being bothered by a strained left hip flexor that prevented her from getting down to low balls.

"I'm going to try to finish in the top five," she said spunkily. "I still have many more tournaments left this year." Which was precisely the problem—too many tournaments, too little time to recover her strength.

Despite her apparent spunkiness, it would take a total overhaul of her conditioning program for her to bounce back if she was to be competitive at the top level again. Mary Joe hired a strength coach and started doing other exercises, including aerobic training and weightlifting to improve her upper body strength. Up until this point, tennis had been her only form of exercise. Although she believes that tennis is a great way to exercise (she told *USA Weekend,*

Mary Joe started an exercise program to improve her strength and endurance.

MARY JOE FERNANDEZ

"Tennis is a sport for a lifetime. You can play it at any age. It's a social sport. . . . You can get good exercise in just an hour"), to be able to compete at the highest levels, she needed to get much stronger.

Working out hard and changing her training regimen paid off. In late 1990 and early 1991, she rose from seventh in the world to fourth among all women tennis players. In August 1991 she briefly surpassed renowned powerhouse Martina Navratilova in the rankings to attain her highest ranking ever (number four) and became the highest-ranked American other than Navratilova and Chris Evert since 1980. In 1992, she reached the semis in the U.S. Open singles before losing to Monica Seles.

Mary Joe had to skip the U.S. Open in 1993, however, because she was hospitalized with her first serious bout of endometriosis, a disease she still lives with. But she

In 1992, Mary Joe reached the semifinals in the U.S. Open singles.

MARY JOE FERNANDEZ

Gigi Fernandez (left) and Mary Joe Fernandez kiss their gold medals after receiving their awards August 8, 1992, for winning the women's doubles event at the Olympic Games in Barcelona, Spain.

bounced back for the 1993 French Open, where she was the fifth-seeded player, and recovered her strength well enough to beat Sabatini in the quarterfinals. This was the longest women's Grand Slam match in the Open era, clocked at 3 hours, 35 minutes. Mary Joe moved on to defeat Arantxa Sanchez Vicario, making it to the finals. She fought courageously against Steffi Graf in the finals before losing 6-4, 2-6, 4-6.

MARY JOE FERNANDEZ

The early '90s also saw her become a top-notch doubles player, and she earned the gold medal in the Olympics at Barcelona with partner Gigi Fernandez (no relation), as well as the bronze medal in singles. Some observers believe Mary Joe is much stronger as a doubles player, and so far she has won more tournaments in doubles play than in singles. She successfully partnered with many different types of players, including Zina Garrison, Pam Shriver, Robin White, and Lindsay Davenport.

Winning the gold in Barcelona, defeating the Spanish doubles pair Arantxa Sanchez Vicario and Conchita Martínez in front of the king and queen of Spain, was a supreme moment of triumph for Mary Joe. She had been asked to play for Spain but had refused. "I'm an American," she said. "I could play for Spain, where my father was born, or the Dominican Republic, where I was born. But . . . it would be difficult to play for another country. I am very patriotic." In fact, she had even been asked to play in the 1988 Olympics for the Dominican Republic but had declined, saying that she would rather represent the U.S. someday.

After winning both a gold and a bronze at Barcelona, Mary Joe said, "For me, this is one of the biggest things ever . . . I've won the Australian, but this is bigger.

▼▼▼▼▼
Winning the gold medal in Barcelona was a supreme moment of triumph for Mary Joe.
▲▲▲▲▲

Mary Joe Fernandez

This is huge." Her father, José, touched the gold medal his daughter had just won and said, "In America, anything is possible."

Some observers claim that Mary Joe is simply "too nice" to become the best in the cutthroat world of championship tennis. A writer for *Sports Illustrated* called her "a frugal, considerate, early-to-bed type [who] has always found it against her nature to do something as reckless as come to the net, much less dictate a point." Critics say she's too skinny and timid to be number one (she's five-feet-ten, 140 pounds). One of the roadblocks she has had to overcome to maintain her competitiveness is mental toughness. As her former coach Tom Gullikson told *Sports Illustrated,* "Graf and Seles go into tournaments expecting to

Mary Joe raises her arms in victory as she scores the winning point.

win. Mary Joe hopes she'll win. . . . When she does, I think she's a little bit surprised."

In a book called *The Courts of Babylon: Tales of Greed and Glory in the Harsh New High-Stakes World of Professional Tennis* (New York: Scribner, 1995), sportswriter Peter Bodo is impressed with Mary Joe's self-possessed, calm attitude. In comparing Mary Joe to international star Gabriela Sabatini, he writes:

> Fernandez seemed firmly grounded. There were several interesting reasons for this. . . . [She] had been raised a Catholic. . . . Up to the age of twenty-two the greatest act of rebellion committed by Fernandez was quietly to renounce her Catholic background and embrace fundamentalist Christianity—a decision that dismayed both of her parents. But I think the portable nature of her new "personal" faith, and the strength she claimed to draw from it, were very powerful assets that helped to make her a well-adjusted young woman reconciled to the demands of her often harsh profession.

Some people think Mary Joe is too nice to be the best in the cutthroat world of championship tennis.

MARY JOE FERNANDEZ

Mary Joe told Bodo that her religion helps motivate her, giving her more of a reason for playing than focusing on tennis for tennis's sake. "There are a lot of corrupt things about tennis, from the amount of money to the lifestyles it creates," she said. She added that she doesn't like the idea of "preaching" her religion but that having faith "helps me to keep everything in perspective, and it helps me to see that the bad times are as much of the ultimate plan as the good times."

For Mary Joe, religion isn't a crutch to lean on but a way of living her life, and being kind to others—even opponents—is part of it. She continues to be a Miss Goody Two-shoes in the sense that she is very concerned about her fellow players. When Monica Seles was stabbed in Berlin in 1994 by a crazed fan of her opponent Steffi Graf, Mary Joe made it a point to stay in touch with Seles for weeks after the horrible incident. After visiting her in the hospital, she repeatedly tried to call Seles, and when she was unable to reach her by phone, she wrote a long letter consoling her wounded rival.

Mary Joe won a prestigious British tournament, the Brighton International, in 1995; she was the first American to win Brighton since Chris Evert had in 1985. She continued her hard work ethic, winning and

"There are a lot of corrupt things about tennis, from the amount of money to the lifestyles it creates."

MARY JOE FERNANDEZ

placing in one tournament after another. In 1995, besides Brighton, she won the singles title at Indian Wells and the doubles titles at Delray Beach, Strasbourg, and Tokyo. In addition, she made it to the finals at Sydney and to the semifinals at Sydney, Oakland, Roland Garros, the Italian Open, and Brighton.

Mary Joe concentrates in the semifinals at the Australian Open in 1995.

Still, Mary Joe's career has had its highs and lows. She had missed much of the 1994 season with an illness, and she injured her back during a match in late 1995. The illness, it turned out, was endometriosis, and since being diagnosed with this disease, Mary Joe has become a spokesperson for increasing awareness of this problem. Endometriosis is a condition in which cells are shed from the lining of the uterus and grow in other organs. "It's not curable, but it's treatable, and one in six women has it," Mary Joe explained. "If you have pain that's more

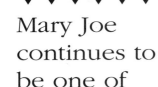

Mary Joe continues to be one of the most popular players on the WTA Tour.

MARY JOE FERNANDEZ

than your monthly cramps, see a doctor right away," she advised.

She played well overall in 1996. The highlight of that year was a repeat victory at the Olympics in Atlanta. With the same partner as in Barcelona in 1992, Gigi Fernandez, Mary Joe received a second gold medal in women's tennis doubles.

In February 1997, she made it to the finals of the Australian Open. One thing was clear: Mary Joe was in tip-top shape to endure the grueling heat of the Australian Open. While other players were suffering dehydration and dropping like flies, she tolerated the intense, 115-plus-degree heat of a court surface that made others wither. One who withered was young opponent Dominique van Roost, who had to forfeit her fourth-round game against Mary Joe due to a pulled abdominal muscle. Going into the tournament, Mary Joe told a reporter, "I love it down here. I love the center court. This is where I reached my first final of a Grand Slam. In the back of my mind I always know that." She made it to the semifinals but lost in that round to 16-year-old Martina Hingis of Switzerland (Hingis just happens to be named after women's tennis great Martina Navratilova, a champion whom Mary Joe had faced in her younger days).

Stronger both physically and mentally, Mary Joe continues to be one of the most popular players on the WTA Tour. She has been around long enough that she's beginning to develop a history. As of late 1996, her singles titles in major tournaments number six, including Indian Wells and Tokyo Indoors; her doubles titles number thirteen, including the Australian and European Opens. By 1997, she had appeared in the

famous English tournament, Wimbledon, ten times. In 1996 she won the doubles title with Lindsay Davenport in the Sydney Open and was a finalist in the Australian Open doubles (also with Davenport, one of her best friends) and at Amelia Island (with Gigi

Left to right: Mary Joe, Gigi Fernandez, Jennifer Capriati and coach Billie Jean King at the Federation Cup tournament, April 1996

MARY JOE FERNANDEZ

Fernandez). She's a perennial seeded player at the great tournaments: the U.S. Open, Wimbledon, the Virginia Slims tournaments, the Lufthansa Cup, and the Tokyo, Australian, French, and Italian Opens.

Medal winners display their awards. Mary Joe repeated her gold medal performance at the 1996 Olympics in Atlanta, Georgia.

Mary Joe has many years before she'll have to retire. Her role model, Chris Evert, retired at 35 and was fourth in the world when she stepped down. "I'm still young and have a lot more years to play," Mary Joe said. "Meanwhile, I'm enjoying myself and everything is going well."

Her attitude toward the sport has always been mature and balanced. She told a writer for *Interview* magazine in 1994 that what separates the top players in the world from others is this: "They know they should be there, at the top, and everybody at that level pretty much plays well all the time. I'm working on that aspect of my game—the visualization or mental aspect. Because in the end, getting there is really about belief, about just having a little more faith in yourself."

Mary Joe is a right-handed player with a two-handed backhand. She originally played in the style similar to that of Chris Evert, only more timid, hitting a lot of baseline shots and not charging the net. She has slowly changed her style of play, adding variety and surprise to her repertoire. After the embarrassing moments early in her full-time career when she suffered from being out of shape, she learned to play more aggressively. Her coach, Harold Solomon, a French Open finalist in 1976, has helped her get tougher on the court.

She was featured on the cover of the December 1996 issue of *Tennis* and penned the story "Win with Variety," in which she gave readers a clinic of shots that she has found successful while playing on tennis's three kinds of surfaces: grass, clay, and hard courts. Indeed, words she uses in the article to describe shots—*flexibility, variety, resil-*

▼▼▼▼▼

Mary Joe is a right-handed player with a two-handed backhand.

▲▲▲▲▲▲

MARY JOE FERNANDEZ

ience—are good words to describe Mary Joe herself.

Mary Joe understands how important it is to be a positive role model, and when her heavy tournament and training schedule permits, she throws herself into causes she believes in. In 1993 she contributed a women's tennis scholarship to Florida International University in Miami. In 1994 she became the national spokesperson for the Cities in Schools / Burger King Academy program, which was aimed at school dropout prevention. She is involved in national and international charities such as Big Brother / Big Sister, the Hunger Project, World Vision

Mary Joe played in the 1996 Olympic Games at the Stone Mountain Tennis Center in Atlanta.

MARY JOE FERNANDEZ

Projects, and Special Olympics. And she was chosen as one of five top current tennis professionals to receive the 1996 Players Who Make a Difference award from *Family Circle*.

When Hurricane Andrew hit south Florida in 1992, Mary Joe worked on behalf of the victims. The hurricane hit her street hard, shifting the roof on her parents' house and ripping up power poles and palm trees. She immediately organized a charity tennis event to benefit the hurricane's less fortunate victims. She and other top tennis players got together for an exhibition, and Mary Joe told ticket buyers, "You're not just going to watch a tennis match, you're going to help rebuild a community."

A great fan of the outdoors and of outdoor sports, Mary Joe's hobbies include golf, wave-running, and waterskiing. A millionaire by the age of 19, she is consistently ranked among the top ten women tennis players in the world and is a household name on four continents, but she remains down-to-earth and concerned about others.

Mary Joe's goal is much the same as it has always been since she picked up a racket: to become the top female player in the world. To do this, she'll have to follow her own advice: "Don't get carried away by what happened or what's going to happen. Stay in the present." At the time of the 1996 Australian Open, her career winnings totaled

▼▼▼▼▼

Mary Joe is involved with national and international charities.

▲▲▲▲▲▲

MARY JOE FERNANDEZ

$4.2 million, but she is rich in other ways, including the kindnesses she shows toward others.

What about life after tennis? After she finishes playing tennis competitively, she wants to become an elementary school teacher. "I would like to get involved with kids," she said, "helping them to read and write."

Mary Joe is not only a talented tennis player, she is a generous humanitarian as well.

INDEX

INDEX